LOCAL RED BOOK

LEGEND

CONTENTS

Redbooks showing the way

Street plans prepared and published by ESTATE PUBLICATIONS, Bridewell House, TENTERDEN, KENT. The Publishers acknowledge the co-operation of the local authorities of towns represented in this atlas.

Ordnance Survey® This product includes mapping data licensed from Ordnance Survey® with the permission of the Controller of Her Majesty's Stationery Office.

www.ESTATE-PUBLICATIONS.co.uk

Legend

═══	Minor Road
▨▨▨	Pedestrianized / Restricted Access
═══	Track
⌐ ⌐	Built Up Area (Centre only)
- - - -	Footpath
∿	Stream
∿	River
Lock	Canal
━━■━━	Railway / Station
●	Post Office
P P+	Car Park / Park & Ride
C	Public Convenience
✛	Place of Worship
→	One-way Street
i	Tourist Information Centre
▲8	Adjoining Pages
	Area Depicting Enlarged Centre
	General Buildings (Centre only)
	Woodland
	Recreation Ground
	Cemetery

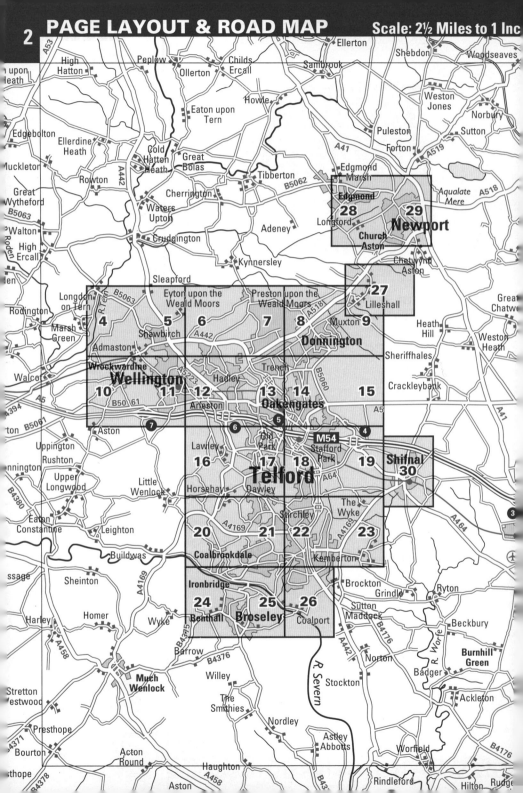

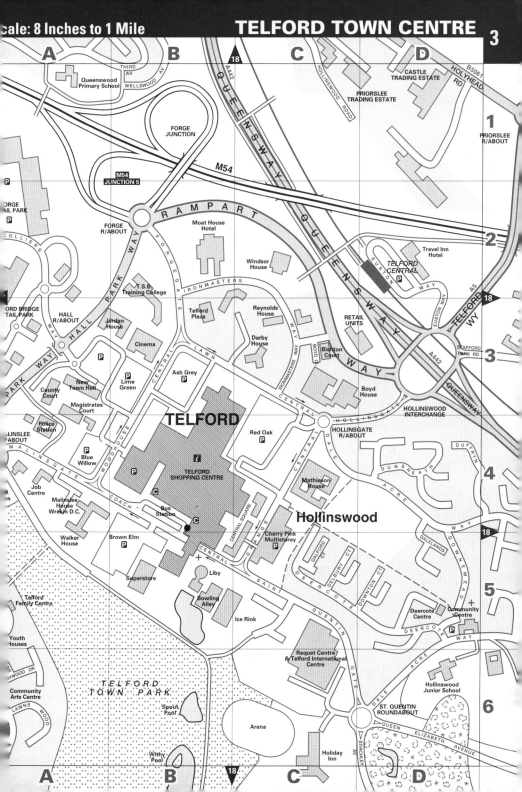

4

A B C D

1

B5063

Mill House

Longdon Hall

Redhouse Farm

Longdon on Tern

The Old Manor

Longdon House

2

Lower Farm

Lower Farm Cottages

Bratton Cottage

The Ranch

LANE

3

River Tern

RUSHMOOR

Brattor Park

Lawn Farm

4

Cheshire Coppice

Bratt

Isombridge Farm

CHESHIRE

Moor Farm

Rushmoor

5

Sewage Works

COPPICE

Cheshire Copp Cottages

Footbridge

Allscott House

LITTLE MDW

6 **Allscott**

Admaston

B4394

A B C D TATION

B4394

A   **B**   **C**   **D**

1

Preston Moor

Crow Brook

2

Wappenshall Moor

5

Mantle
Covert

Kinley
Farm

Wappenshall
Covert

3

Eyton Hall

Wappenshall

Wappenshall
Bridge

Hurley Brook

Park
Covert

Wappenshall
Farm

4

arm

5

Wheatley
Grange

A442

Apley Cottages

WAY   **Q**   **U**   **E**   **E**   **N**   **S**   **W**   **A**   **Y**

5

Apley Pool

GOSHAWK
DR

SPARROWHAWK
WY

PEREGRINE

Pump
Wood

GOLDCREST
GRO

OSPREY GRO

WOSPREY GRO

WAY

CHICHESTER
CL

MANCHESTER

BRANDON
GRO

BEAUFORT DR

MONTGOMERY

LAWS

DR

LEEGOMERY
R/ABOUT

QUEENSWA

INDUSTRIAL
ESTATE

WAY

Apley Castle Park

PINTAIL DR

EIDER
GRO

BARNES

UNDERLAM

WALLIS DR

BADER

AUSTER

SPRUCE
DR

BERBERIS RD

CACTUS DR

AVENUE

WOODPECKER
CL

HADLEY

OKEHAMPTON

CARLISLE

PORCHESTER

HEDINGHAM
CL

SANDAL
CL

6

CASTLE   APLEY

Apley
Castle

SHOVELLER
DR

WIGEON
GRO

MERGANSER

ALBACORE
RD

BLENHEIM
RD

SAXON CT

LEEGATE

CLEMATIS DR

ANCHORIA DR

HADLEY
GDNS

PARK

HADLEY

ROAD

CASTLE AGRE RD

DOVER RD

DORCHESTER
RD

WARWICK WAY

A5223

DRIVE

WHITC

HELLINS
ST

THE PRINCESS ROYAL
(TELFORD DISTRICT GENERAL)
HOSPITAL

PASTEUR
WY

SHELLDUCK

CURIE

CAVELL

ELESA

FLEMING WY

NIGHTINGALE

POOL
LANE

FARM
CLOSE

LAWTON
RM

ROYAL
OAK
DR

School

ANSON
DR

Leegomery

12

Comm
Centre

P

A   **B**   **C**   **D**

E F G H

School

Preston upon the
Weald Moors

Preston
Trust Homes

Humber Brook

1 Lubstr
Park

HUMBER EAST VIEW

HUMBER LA

HUMBER

2

Hoo

Hoo Farm
Nature Park

Hoo Hall

Crow Brook

Hoo Farm

Barracks

8

3

Horton

Horton Farm

HORTON LANE

HORTON COURT
1-28

BASE
ORDNANCE
DEPOT

4

Hortonwood 50

CROWBROOK
R/ABOUT

8

5

QUEENSWAY

Hadley Park
House Hotel

KIN

Nursery
School

HADLEY PARK
ROUNDABOUT

ORCHARD
FARM
R/ABOUT

HORTONWOOD

Works

30

31

32

33

35

37

HORTONWOOD

HORTONWOOD

HORTON

HORTONWOOD

HORTONWOOD ROUNDABOUT

NEW TRENCH RD

A518

NEW

6

1

2

10

7

A442

QUEENSWAY

HORTON LA

A518

NEW TRENCH ROAD

HORTON
RD

TRENCH RD

PRESTON

VIEWLANDS

GROVE

WOMBRIDGE

BROADWAY

MILL

WANWOOD

GORDON

CHURCH

WOODHO

CRES

School

13

E F G H

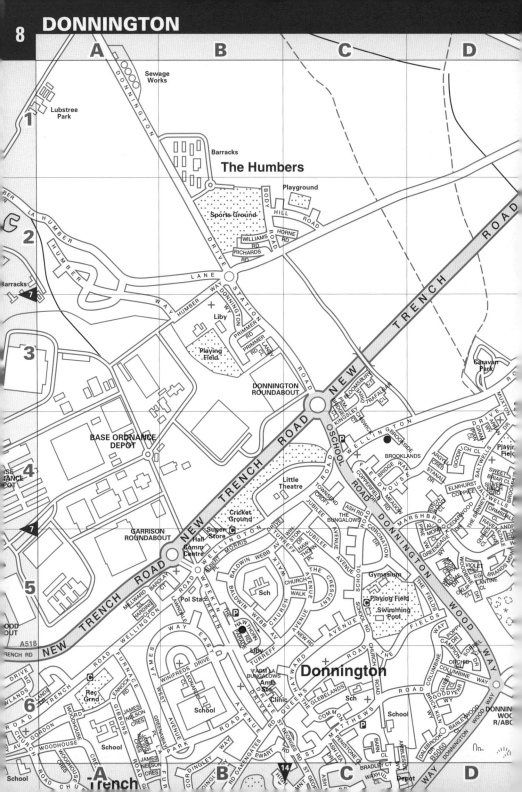

Lilleshall

Honnington

Muxton

E   F   G   H

NEW TRENCH RD

KYNNERSLEY DRIVE

A518

WELLINGTON RD

WELLINGTON RD

WILLMOOR LANE

LANE

EAST

HILLSIDE

ROCK ACRES

ST MICHAEL'S CL

CHURCH MDW

Monument

School

Cricket Grnd

Youth Centre

OLD FARM LA

Lilleshall Hall Farm

Cemy

ROAD

ABBEY

CHURCH

School

YEW TREE DR

The Old Hall

WELLINGTON

NELSON CL

MERRINGTON RD

Honnington Grange

ROAD

Lilleshall Grange

The Oaks

ABBEY

Grange Cottages

Remains of Augustinian Abbey

ROAD

LILYHURST RD

Abbey Farm

Sulphur Piece Plantation

GRANVILLE DR

THE PADDOCK

MUXTON LANESIDE

STERLEY GRO

MALICE CL

MILLER CL

ABLES CL

LYTTON

HOLLAND DR

ASHBROOK

LYTHAM GREEN

Sch

CANTERBURY CL

WINCHESTER DR

WEYBOURNE WK

LYTHAM WAY

WAY

CALDER CL

LANE

Muxton

The Shropshire P.H.

Golf Driving Range

Club House

Golf Course

New Lodge

PJ

27

27

15

E   F   G   H

1

2

3

4

5

6

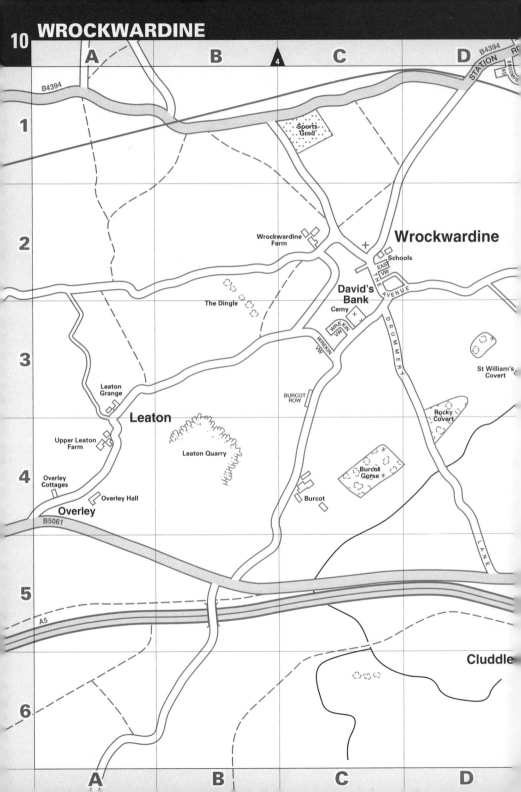

A   **B**   ▲ 4   **C**   **D**

B4394
STATION RD
BROOMFIE
RD

1

B4394

Sports Grnd

2

Wrockwardine Farm

Wrockwardine

Schools

EAST VW

THE AVENUE

David's Bank

The Dingle

Cemy

WREKIN VW

DRUMMERY

3

BURCOT ROW

St William's Covert

Leaton Grange

Rocky Covert

Leaton

Upper Leaton Farm

Leaton Quarry

Burcot Gorse

4

Overley Cottages

Overley Hall

Burcot

Overley

B5061

LANE

5

A5

Cluddle

6

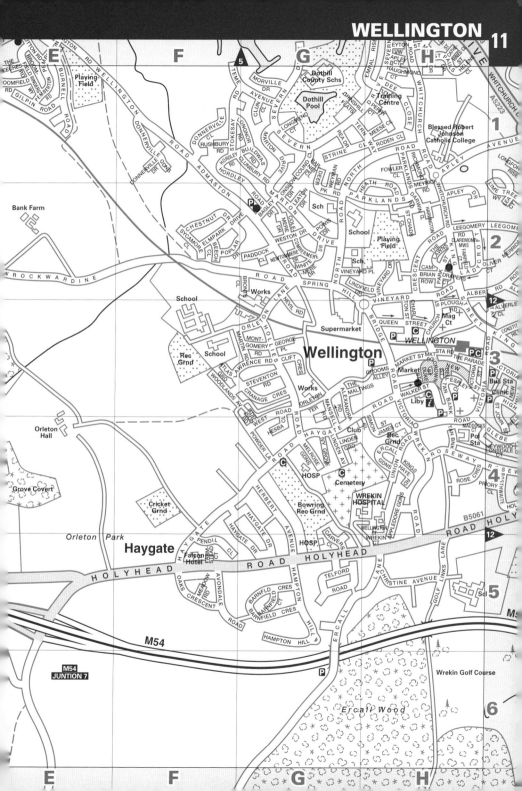

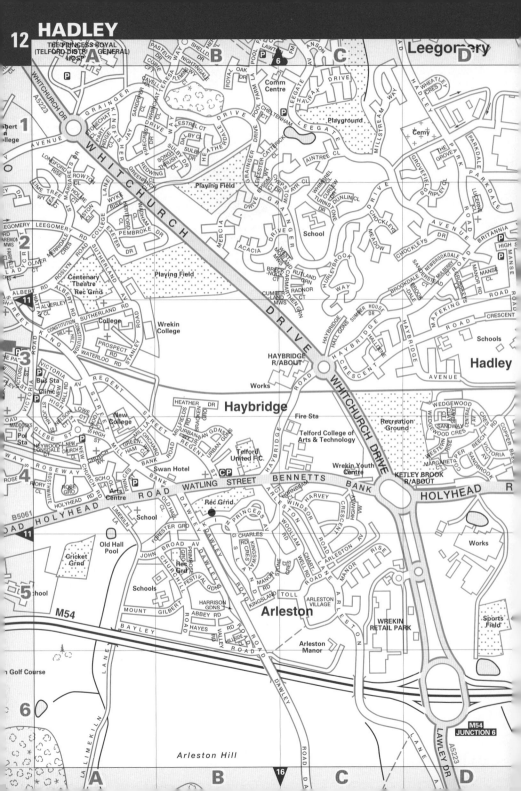

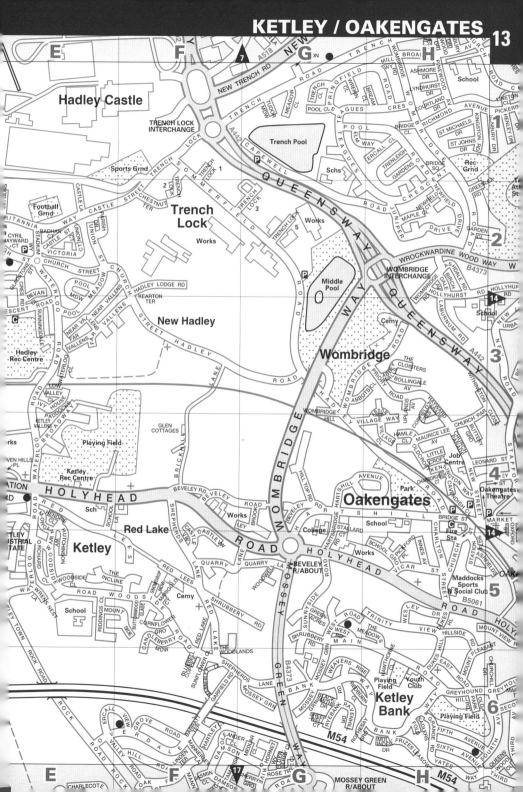

E   F   ▲9   G   New L   H

1

P

GRANVILLE ROAD

GRANVILLE

GRANGE

Ferndale Farm

Granville Country Park

ROAD

2

Cooper's Coppice

WOODHOUSE

Dawes Bower

Woodhouse Farm

LANE

3

Watling Street Grange

4

GRANGE

EKILN BANK UNDABOUT

VXACONA Roman Settlement (Site of)

WATLING STREET   ROMAN ROAD   A5

LANE

Redhill

Upper Woodhouse Farm

Woodgreen

5

Medical Centre

Sch

WEST MINSTER WAY

Rec Grnd

ELTHAM DR

YORK

WATERLOW CL

CHANCERY PK

HEREFORD AVE

SOUTH WELL ROAD

ELY

VALE

FINCH

SALISBURY

MAYFAIR GRO

WYNDHAM

LORD GRO

CLIFFORD CL

HIGHGROVE MDWS

CAMELLIA DR

LICHFIELD CL

6

The Woodhouse

CASTLE FARM WAY

WOODHOUSE LANE

CHILCOMBE DR

LILYVALE CL

KEW GDNS

KESWORTH DR

B5060

E   F   ▼19   G   H

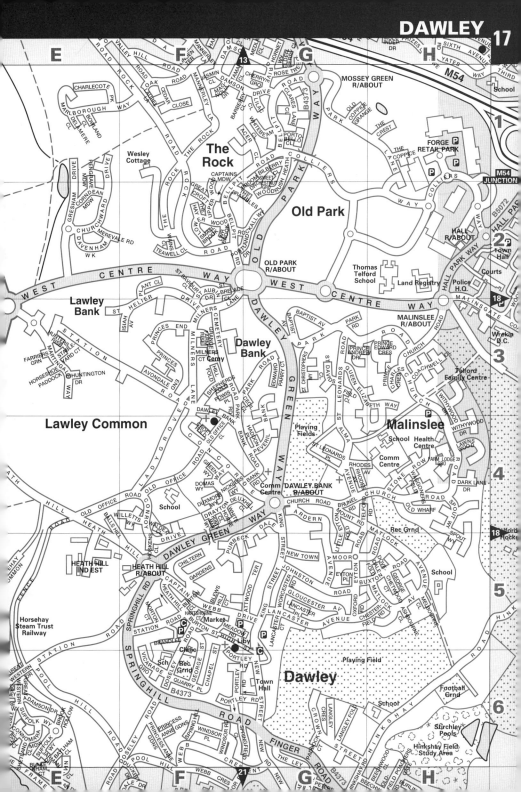

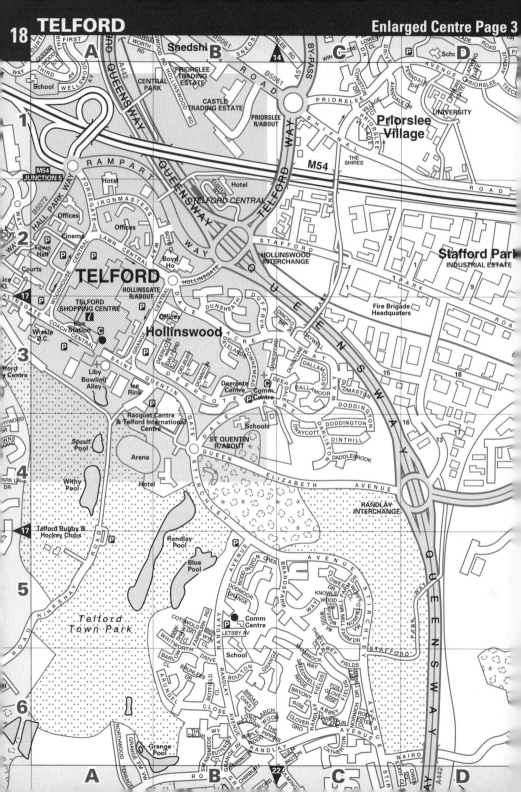

TELFORD

Hollinswood

Priorslee Village

Stafford Park
INDUSTRIAL ESTATE

Telford Town Park

Shedshi

UNIVERSITY

THE SHIRES

M54

M54 JUNCTION 5

RAMPART WAY

QUEENSWAY

TELFORD WAY

PRIORSLEE

Hotel

Hotel

TELFORD CENTRAL

Town Hall

Cinema

Offices

Offices

Courts

Wrekin D.C.

Bus Station

TELFORD SHOPPING CENTRE

HOLLINSGATE R/ABOUT

PRIORSLEE TRADING ESTATE

CASTLE TRADING ESTATE

CENTRAL PARK

PRIORSLEE R/ABOUT

HOLLINSWOOD INTERCHANGE

Fire Brigade Headquaters

Liby Bowling Alley

Ice Rink

Racquet Centre & Telford International Centre

Deercote Centre

Comm Centre

Schools

ST QUENTIN R/ABOUT

Spout Pool

Arena

Withy Pool

Hotel

RANDLAY INTERCHANGE

QUEEN ELIZABETH AVENUE

Telford Rugby & Hockey Clubs

Randlay Pool

Blue Pool

DODMOOR GRANGE

Comm Centre

School

KNOWLE WOOD

Grange Pool

A442

QUEENSWAY

E **F** **G** **H**

15

1

Works

RICOH

Priorslee Balancing Lake

Factory

M54
JUNCTION 4

2

CASTLE FARM
INTERCHANGE

M54

30

7

6

6

5

6

Taggs Rough

Leisure
Park

3

4

10

Knowl Wood

11

4

Obelisk

NAIRD
ROUNDABOUT

Blythbury
Farm

Haughton
Farm

A464
PRIOR

Works

30

LFORD SCIENCE
CHNOLOGY PARK

5

Nedge Hill

Shaw Farm

LANE SHAW

6

A4169
BRID

E **F** **G** **H**

23

CASTLE FARM WAY

WOODHOUSE LANE

B5060

PRIORSLEE ROAD

HAUGHTON LANE

NAIRD LANE

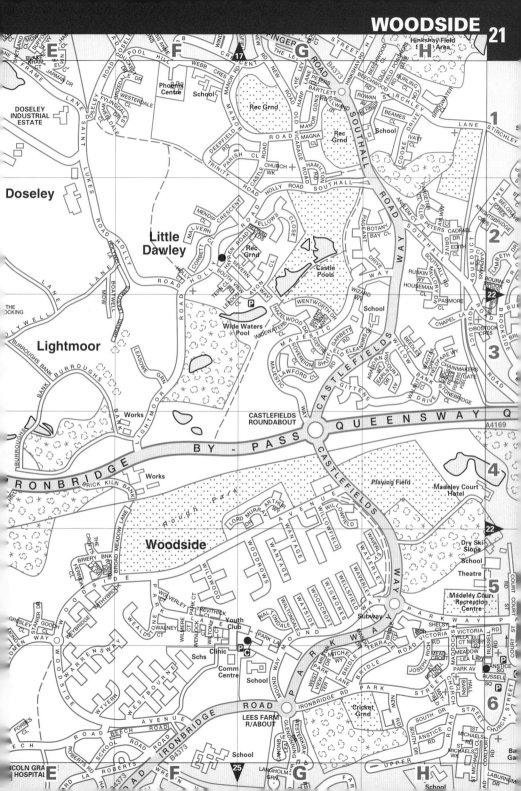

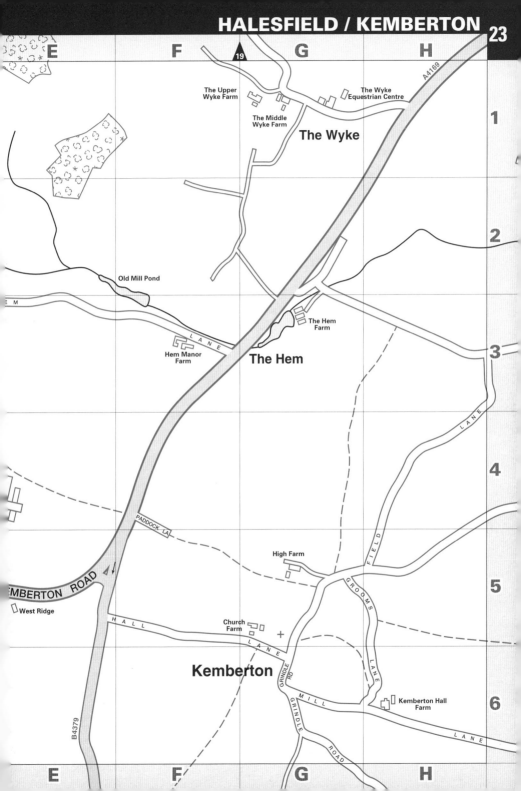

E F G H

1

The Upper Wyke Farm

The Wyke Equestrian Centre

A4169

The Middle Wyke Farm

The Wyke

2

Old Mill Pond

The Hem Farm

M

L A N E

Hem Manor Farm

The Hem

L A N E

3

4

PADDOCK LA

FIELD

High Farm

GROOMS

5

EMBERTON ROAD

West Ridge

HALL

Church Farm

LANE

LANE

Kemberton

GRINDLE RD

MILL

Kemberton Hall Farm

6

B4379

GRINDLE ROAD

LANE

E F G H

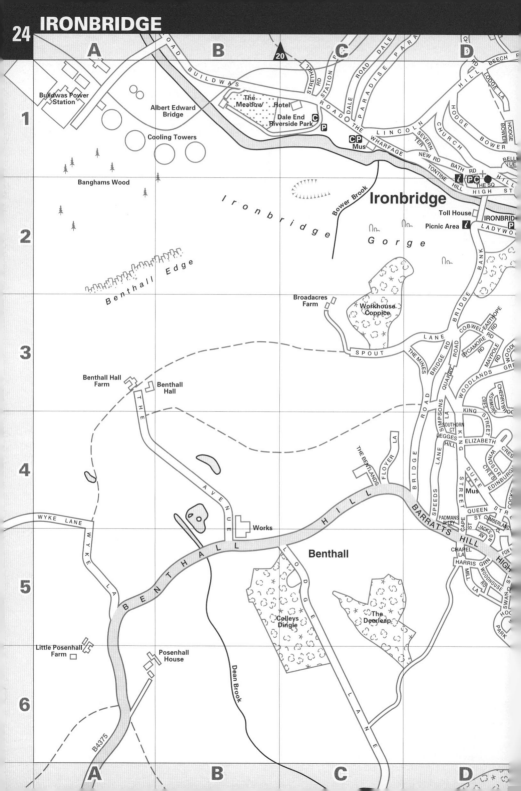

A B C D

IRONBRIDGE

Buildwas Power Station

Albert Edward Bridge

Cooling Towers

Banghams Wood

The Meadow Hotel

Dale End Riverside Park

ROAD BUILDWAS

STRETHILL RD

STATION RD

DALE ROAD

PARADISE DALE

THE WHARFAGE

SEVERN

LINCOLN

NEW RD

CHURCH

BATH RD

TONTINE HILL

HIGH ST

THE SQ

BEECH HILL

LODGE LA

HODGE BOWER

HODGE BOWER

BELLE VUE

Mus

CP

P

Ironbridge

Gorge

Bower Brook

Toll House

Picnic Area

IRONBRIDGE

LADYWO

Broadacres Farm

Workhouse Coppice

SPOUT LANE

THE MINES

BRIDGE ROAD

QUARRY ROAD

COBWELL ROAD

EASTHOPE RD

SYCAMORE RD

MAYPOLE RD

WOODLANDS

BRIDGE BANK

Benthall Edge

Benthall Hall Farm

Benthall Hall

THE AVENUE

KING STREET

SIMPSONS LANE

SOUTHORN CT

LEGGES HILL

ELIZABETH CRES

WINDSOR CRES

DUKE STREET

ASHMORE CRES

CHERRYTREE HILL

KING STREET

Mus

WYKE LANE

WYKE LA

BENTHALL

Works

THE BENTLANDS

FLOYER LA

BRIDGE ROAD

SPEEDS LANE

PADMANS ALLEY

QUEEN ST

CAPE ST

JACK'D

CUMBERLAND AV

FOX

BARRATTS HILL

HIGH

Benthall

Colleys Dingle

The Deerleap

LODGE

CHAPEL LA

HARRIS GRN

WOODHOUSE

MILL LA

SWAN

PARK

Little Posenhall Farm

Posenhall House

Dean Brook

LANE

B4375

A B C D

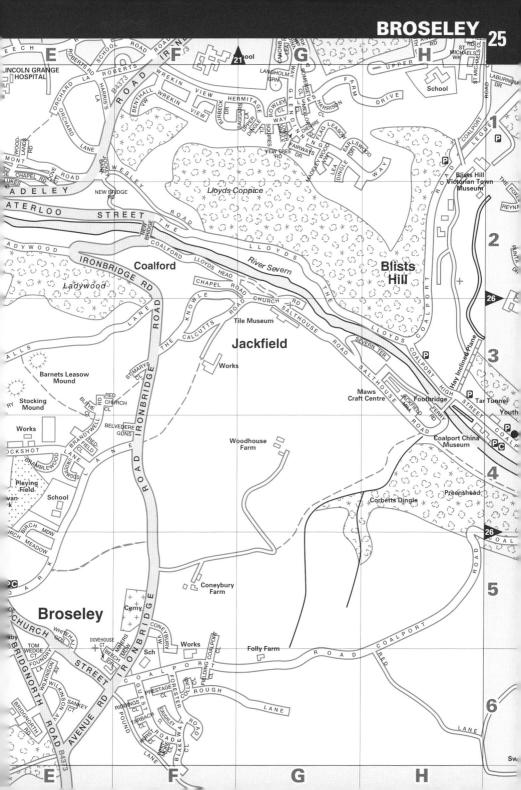

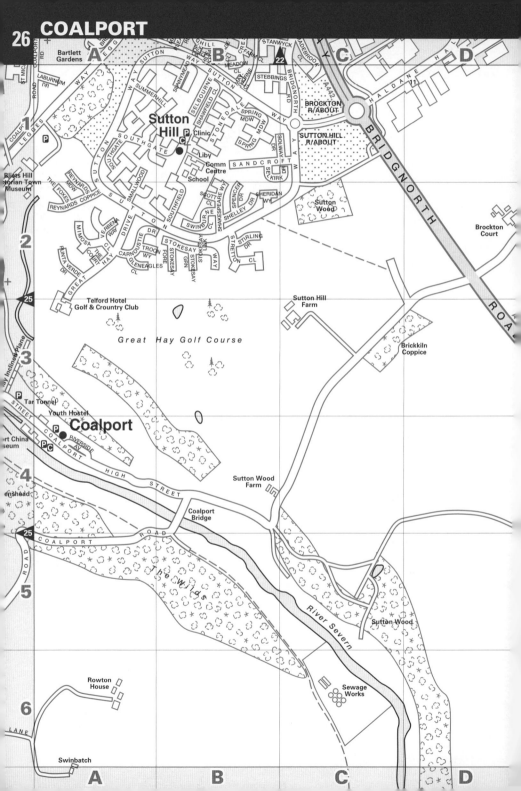

A **B** **C** **D**

Bartlett Gardens

ST MICH
COALPORT RD

BLEGG

BROAD CHILL

STANWYCK

MEADBROOK

A442

BRIDGNORTH ROAD

HALDANE

LABURNUM DR

SUMMERHILL

SUTTON

SUNNYMEAD

MEADOW

CREAM

STEBBINGS

BROCKTON R/ABOUT

COALPORT RD

LEGGES WAY

P

SELBOURNE CL

SHAWFIELD CL

SPRING MDW

BRIDGNORTH RD

SUTTON HILL R/ABOUT

Sutton Hill

P Clinic

STONEDALE

SPRING

SOLWAY DR

Liby

SOUTHGATE

SANDCROFT

SE KIRK

Brockton Court

Rliets Hill ctorian Town Museum

REYNARDS MDW

THE FOXES

Comm Centre

School

SMALLWOOD

SOUTHFIELD

SCOTT CL

SHAKESPEARE CL

SPENCER DR

SHELLEY

SHERIDAN WY

Sutton Wood

REYNARDS COPPICE

MIMOSA CL

PUNTA VERDE DR

THE COURT

VERBENA WAY

DRIVE

GREAT HAY

CARNOUSTIE DR

TROON WY

GLENEAGLES CL

STOKESAY FORE

STOKESAY GRN

SWINO

NICHOLS WAY

STIRLING CL

STRETTON CL

Telford Hotel Golf & Country Club

Sutton Hill Farm

Great Hay Golf Course

Brickkiln Coppice

ay Inclined Plane

P Tar Tonnel

Youth Hostel

Coalport

RIVERSIDE AV

P
P

COALPORT

HIGH STREET

Sutton Wood Farm

rt China seum

enshead

Coalport Bridge

COALPORT ROAD

25

ROAD

The Winds

River Severn

Sutton Wood

Rowton House

Sewage Works

LANE

Swinbatch

A **B** **C** **D**

Little Hales Manor Farm

LILLESHALL HALL NATIONAL SPORTS CENTRE

Abbey Wood

Treeline Plantation

New House Farm

Remains of Augustinian

WILLMOOR LANE

LANE

Lilleshall

Youth Centre

OLD FARM LA

Lilleshall Hall Farm

School

Cricket Grnd

Monument

CHURCH MDW

Cemy

Lilleshall Grange

The Old Hall

School

ROCK

ST MICHAELS CL

ROCK ACRES

HILLSIDE

EAST

LIMEKILN LANE

BLACK LANE

Brockton Leasows

CHESWELL DRIVE

A518 WELLINGTON ROAD

WELLINGTON RD

YEW TREE DR

ORCHARD

ABBEY ROAD

ABBEY ROAD

he Oaks

ton

A   B   C   D

1

B5062

SHREWSBURY ROAD

LONGWITHY LANE

WOODRIDGE CL

MENTONE CRES

CHETWYND ROAD

CHETWYND ROAD

Newport Showground

2

FT RD

STACKYARD LANE

SHREWSBURY ROAD

NEWPORT RD

NEWPORT LANE

NEWPORT

ROAD

HILLSIDE

PIPERS LANE

MANOR RD

SCHOOL RD

TURNERS

CONNERS LA

STREET

ROBIN

BAYLEY HILLSIDE

3

KILVERT CL

ST PETERS WY

ROCK LA

HIGH

Sch

Edgmond

Windy Meadows Farm

Tickethouse Lock

Re Gr

Sewage Works

4

Vauxhall House

R
O
A
D

5

Bridge Farm

Brook Cottage

Longford

L
O
N
G
F
O
R
D

Longford Hall

Pool Covert

Longford Mill Farm

6

Mill Wood

A   B   C   D

E **F** **G** **H**

1

2

3

4

5

6

Park Pool

Newport
Rugby Club

Blue House
Barns

DGMOND

ROAD

GREEN

LANE

Islington

Playing
Fields

Shropshire Union Canal Newport Branch

Sch

Offs

BROOK
HO

Swim
Pool

Park

Fire Sta

School

Market

School

Liby

BURGAGE
CT

Supermarket

BELLMANS
YARD

Fitness
Centre

High
Meadows

Club House

Golf
Course

Rec Grnd

Pol
Sta

Clinic

School

Cricket
Grnd

School

Audley
House

School

Cerny

AUDLEY AVENUE
INDUSTRIAL
ESTATE

Schs

NEWPORT

SPRINGFIELD
INDUSTRIAL
ESTATE

Refuse Disposal
Point

Millwood
Mere

Greenfield
Ter

BY - PASS

Playing
Field

**Church
Aston**

Chetwynd Aston

Sch

Little Hales
Road

Aston
Manor

E **F** **G** **H**

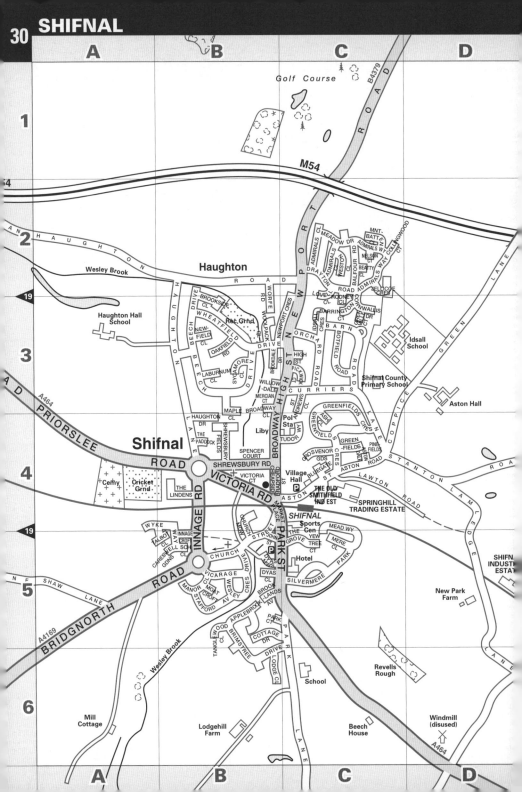

Golf Course

B4379

M54

Haughton

Wesley Brook

Haughton Hall School

PRIORSLEE

A464

ROAD

Shifnal

SHREWSBURY RD

Cricket Grnd

Cemy

THE LINDENS

VICTORIA RD

INNAGE RD

BRIDGNORTH

A4169

ROAD

SHAW LANE

Mill Cottage

Lodgehill Farm

School

Idsall School

Shifnal County Primary School

Aston Hall

Village Hall

THE OLD SMITHFIELD IND EST

SPRINGHILL TRADING ESTATE

SHIFNAL

Sports Cen

Hotel

New Park Farm

Revells Rough

Windmill (disused)

A464

Beech House

SHIFNAL INDUSTRIAL ESTATE

The Index includes some
names for which there is
insufficient space on the
maps. These names are
indicated by an * and are
followed by the nearest
adjoining thoroughfare.

Abbey Ct Shopping Arc	
TF10	29 F3
Abbey Flds TF3	18 C6
Abbey Rd,	
Newport TF10	9 F2
Abbey Rd, Telford TF1	12 B5
Abbey Walls TF3	13 H3
Abbots Cl TF2	13 G3
Abdon Ct TF2	13 H4
Abelia Way TF2	15 E6
Abraham Cl TF3	22 A2
Acacia Dr TF1	12 B2
Acer Cl TF3	17 F1
Acorn Way TF5	5 F5
Adams Cres TF10	29 E3
Adamson Dr TF4	17 E6
Addison Rd TF1	11 G3
Admaston Rd TF1	11 F1
Admaston Spa TF5	5 F5
Admirals Cl TF1	30 C2
Admirals Way TF11	30 C2
Ainsdale Dr TF2	18 C1
Aintree Cl TF1	12 C1
Albacore Rd TF1	6 B6
Albert Pl TF2	8 B5
Albert Rd TF1	11 H2
Albert St TF4	14 B4
Albion Hill TF2	14 B4
Albion St TF2	14 B4
Alder Mead Cl TF5	5 E6
Alderslee Cl TF2	14 D5
Aldridge Cl TF2	14 D6
Alexandra Rd TF1	11 G3
Allertons Mdw TF5	5 F5
Alma Av TF4	17 G4
Almond Ct TF2	8 D4
Alton Gro TF10	29 E5
Amberley Cl TF1	12 A3
Ambleside Way TF2	8 C6
Andreas Dr TF2	8 D5
Anslem Ct TF3	21 H2
Anson Dr TF1	6 C6
Apprentice Rd TF7	21 H6
Apprentice Sq TF7	22 A6
Apsley Av TF1	11 H1
Apsley Castle TF1	5 H6
Apsley Ct TF1	5 H6
Apsley Dr TF1	11 H2
Applebrook TF11	30 B5
Appledore Gdns TF1	11 H5
Aqualate Cl TF10	29 G2
Aqueduct La TF3	21 H2
Aqueduct Rd TF3	21 H3
Aragorn Way TF4	21 H3
Aralia Cl TF2	15 E6
Ardern Av TF4	17 G4
Argyll Cres TF2	8 D4
Arleston Av TF1	12 C5
Arleston Ct TF1	12 B4
Arleston La TF1	12 B4
Arleston Village TF1	12 C5
Armstrong Ct TF7	21 E5
Arran Way TF2	8 D4
Arrow Rd TF5	5 G4
Arthur Way TF7	21 G4
Arundel Cl TF3	18 B6
Ascot Cl TF11	30 C4
Ash Lea Dr TF2	8 C6
Ash Rd TF2	8 C4
Ashbourne Cl TF4	17 H5
Ashdale Rd TF2	13 H2
Ashdown La*,	
Stafford Shopping Centre	
TF3	3 B4
Ashfields TF2	13 H5

Ashlea Dr TF2	14 C1
Ashley Rd TF2	14 C5
Ashmore Cres TF12	24 D3
Ashmore Dr TF2	13 H1
Ashworth Way TF10	29 F4
Aspen Way,	
Newport TF10	29 F4
Aspen Way,	
Telford TF5	5 G5
Aston Cl TF1	12 A2
Aston Dale TF11	30 C4
Aston Dr TF10	29 E4
Aston Rd TF11	30 C4
Aston St TF11	30 C4
Athol Dr TF2	14 B5
Atlas Gro TF1	11 F3
Attingham Cl TF3	22 C2
Attwood Ter TF4	17 G5
Audley Av TF10	29 G4
Audley Av Ind Est	
TF10	29 H4
Audley Ct TF10	29 G4
Audley Rd TF10	29 F3
Auster Cl TF1	6 C6
Avenue Rd,	
Broseley TF12	25 E6
Avenue Rd,	
Newport TF10	29 F4
Avenue Rd South	
TF10	29 F4
Avon Cl TF4	21 G2
Avondale,	
Newport TF10	29 F2
Avondale, Telford TF4	17 F3
Avondale Rd TF1	11 F5
Aylwin Ct TF3	21 H2
Ayr Cl TF1	12 C2
Bader Cl TF1	6 C6
Badger Cl TF3	22 A1
Badhan Ct TF1	13 E2
Bagley Dr TF1	11 G2
Baldwin Webb Av TF2	8 B5
Balfour Rd TF11	30 C2
Balls Hill TF4	17 E4
Balls La TF8	25 E3
Bank Rd, Dawley TF4	17 F4
Bank Rd,	
Wellington TF1	12 A4
Bank Way TF2	13 G6
Baptist Av TF4	17 G3
Barber St TF12	24 D5
Barberry Cl TF3	17 F1
Barclay Ct TF1	8 A5
Barkers Ct TF7	22 A6
Barleywood Cl TF2	8 D6
Barlow Cl TF3	18 B6
Barn Cl TF2	8 C6
Barn Rd TF11	30 C3
Barnes Wallis Dr TF1	6 B6
Barnet Cl TF1	11 G1
Barnfield Cres TF1	11 G5
Barnfield Ct TF1	11 G5
Barnmeadow Cl TF10	29 G3
Barnmeadow Rd TF10	29 G3
Barrack La TF10	27 B1
Barratt Ter TF3	13 F6
Barratts Hill TF12	24 D4
Barrington Ct TF11	30 C3
Bartholomew Rd TF4	16 D3
Bartlett Rd TF4	21 G1
Bath Rd TF8	24 D1
Bayley Hills TF10	28 B3
Bayley Rd TF1	11 G2
Baylham Cl TF4	17 E6
Bayswater Cl TF2	15 E5
Beaconsfield TF3	22 B2
Beames Cl TF4	21 H1
Beatty Cl TF1	30 C2
Beaufort Cl TF1	6 C5
Beaumaris Rd TF10	29 E3
Beckbury Dr TF3	22 A2
Bedstone Cl TF3	22 B2

Beech Cl,	
Newport TF10	29 F5
Beech Cl, Telford TF1	11 F2
Beech Dr,	
Broseley TF12	25 E6
Beech Dr, Shifnal TF11	30 B3
Beech Rd TF7	21 E6
Beechfields Way TF10	29 F1
Beechwood Cl TF4	21 H1
Beechwood Rd TF4	21 G1
Beedles Cl TF3	21 H3
Belgrave Cres TF3	22 A2
Bell St TF1	11 H3
Belle Vue Rd TF8	24 D1
Bellmans Yd TF10	29 F4
Bellpit Rd TF3	17 F2
Belmont Rd TF4	21 G1
Belvedere Gdns TF12	25 E4
Bembridge TF3	22 B2
Bennett Rd TF7	22 B5
Bennetts Bank TF1	12 B4
Benthall Hill TF12	24 A5
Benthall Vw TF7	25 F1
Berberis Rd TF1	6 C6
Berkeley Cl TF2	15 E4
Berwyn Cl TF3	18 B5
Betnell Gro TF7	21 H6
Bevan Cl TF1	13 E3
Beveley Rd TF2	13 F4
Bilberry Cl TF3	17 G1
Birbeck Dr TF7	25 F1
Birch Dale Av TF2	13 H2
Birch Mdw TF12	25 E5
Birch Row TF12	25 E5
Birchlee Cl TF2	14 D5
Birchmore TF3	22 A2
Birchwood Cl TF2	8 D4
Bishopdale TF3	22 A3
Blackheni Cl TF10	29 E4
Blacksmiths Dr TF2	13 G6
Blackstone Dr TF2	14 B4
Blackthorn Grn TF5	5 G5
Blakemore TF3	22 B3
Blakenham Ct TF4	17 E6
Blakeway Cl TF12	25 F6
Blenheim Rd TF1	6 B6
Blews Hill Ct TF4	17 F5
Blithe Cl TF12	25 E3
Bloomsbury Ct TF2	8 C3
Blue House Barns TF10	29 E1
Bluebell Coppice TF1	13 F6
Bluegate TF11	30 C4
Blythe Gdns TF2	14 C2
Board Cl TF2	14 C1
Boddington Cres TF3	18 B5
Body Rd TF2	8 B2
Bollingale Av TF1	13 H3
Boningale Cl TF3	22 B2
Boscobel Cl TF3	22 C2
Bostock Cl TF5	5 E6
Bostock Cres TF3	21 H3
Botany Bay Cl TF4	21 H2
Botfield Cl TF3	18 B6
Botfield Rd TF1	30 C3
Boughey Rd TF10	29 E4
Boulton Grange TF3	18 B4
Bournbrook Gdns TF3	21 H2
Bournside Dr TF3	22 A3
Bourton Cl TF3	22 B2
Bowland Cl TF3	17 E1
Boyd Cl TF3	3 C3
Bracken Gro TF1	12 B4
Bracken Way TF10	29 F2
Bradford St TF11	30 B4
Bradley Cl TF4	14 C1
Bradley Rd TF2	14 C1
Brakenfield TF3	22 A3
Bramblewood TF12	25 E4
Bramwell Cl TF2	14 B4
Brandlee TF4	17 F5
Brandon Av TF5	5 F5
Brandon Gro TF1	6 B5
Brands Mdw TF2	8 D5

Brandsfarm Way TF3	18 C5
Brandywell Rd TF12	25 E4
Bratton Rd TF5	5 E6
Bream Cl TF2	13 H1
Brecknock Cl TF1	12 B2
Brereton TF3	22 B3
Briarwood TF3	22 A2
Brick Kiln Bank TF7	21 E4
Brick Kiln Way TF2	8 D6
Brickhill La TF1	13 F4
Bridge Bank TF8	24 D3
Bridge Cl TF2	13 H1
Bridge Rd,	
Broseley TF12	24 D4
Bridge Rd,	
Horsehay TF4	16 D6
Bridge Rd,	
Wellington TF1	11 H3
Bridge Sq TF2	13 H1
Bridge St TF2	13 H4
Bridge Way TF3	8 C4
Bridgnorth Rd,	
Broseley TF12	25 E5
Bridgnorth Rd,	
Shifnal TF11	30 A6
Bridgnorth Rd,	
Telford TF1	22 A4
Bridgwater Cl TF4	21 H1
Bridgwood TF3	22 B2
Bridle Ct TF7	21 H5
Bridle Ter TF7	21 G6
Briery Bank TF7	21 E5
Briggs Way TF2	14 B3
Brimstree Dr TF11	30 B5
Brindleyford TF3	22 A3
Britannia Way TF1	12 D2
Broad Meadow La TF7	21 F5
Broad Oaks TF3	18 B6
Broadstone Mws TF4	21 G3
Broadway,	
Newport TF10	29 G3
Broadway,	
Shifnal TF11	30 B4
Broadway, Telford TF1	13 E4
Broadway Av TF2	7 H6
Broadway Cl TF11	30 B3
Brockford Glade TF1	5 F6
Brockton Way TF7	22 B4
Brockwood Copse TF1	5 F6
Bromley Way TF2	14 B5
Bronte Cl TF1	11 G2
Brook Ho TF10	29 E3
Brook Hollow TF4	17 E6
Brook Mdw TF5	5 F5
Brook Rd TF7	22 B5
Brookdale TF1	12 C2
Brookdale Dr TF11	30 B3
Brooklands TF2	8 C4
Brooklands Av TF11	30 B5
Brookside TF2	8 C4
Brookside Av,	
Newport TF10	29 E5
Brookside Av,	
Telford TF3	22 A2
Brookside Cl TF11	30 B3
Brookvale Rd TF2	14 D6
Broom Dr TF3	17 G2
Broomfield Cl TF10	29 E3
Broomfield Pl TF10	29 E3
Broomfield Rd,	
Newport TF10	29 E3
Broomfield Rd,	
Telford TF3	5 E6
Broomhurst Way TF2	8 D4
Brunel Rd TF4	17 G4
Brunlees Dr TF3	18 B6
Bryony Rise TF3	18 C6
Bryony Way TF2	14 D6
Buckingham Cres TF2	22 A2
Buildwas Bank TF8	20 A4
Buildwas Rd,	
Ironbridge TF8	20 A5

Buildwas Rd,	
Wellington TF1	11 G1
Bullrush Glade TF2	14 B3
Burcot Row TF6	10 C3
Burford TF3	22 B3
Burgage Ct TF10	29 F4
Burleigh Cl TF3	22 B2
Burlington Cl TF4	21 H1
Burnell Rd TF5	11 E1
Burnside TF3	22 A3
Burnthall La TF7	22 A6
Burroughs Bank TF4	21 E4
Burton Cl TF4	17 F5
Burton St TF4	17 F5
Burtondale TF3	22 B3
Bush Cl TF1	5 G6
Buttercup Cl TF3	18 B6
Buttermere Dr TF2	14 C6
Buttery Gro TF2	13 H4
Buttonwood Glade TF1	13 F5
Butts Rd TF5	5 F4
Buxton Rd TF4	17 G5
Cactus Dr TF1	6 C6
Cadfael Dr TF3	21 H2
Cadman Dr TF2	14 D6
Calcott TF3	22 C1
Calcutts Rd TF8	25 F3
Calder Cl TF2	9 E6
Caldercrofts TF10	29 F2
Calluna Dr TF2	15 E6
Calverhall TF3	22 C1
Cambrian Row TF1	11 H2
Camellia Dr TF2	15 E6
Campion Dr TF2	8 D5
Canal Side TF2	14 B1
Candleberry Mdw TF1	13 F6
Canonbie Lea TF7	21 G6
Canongate TF2	14 A5
Canterbury Cl TF2	9 E5
Cape St TF12	24 D5
Capewell Rd TF2	13 G1
Cappoquin Dr TF2	14 B3
Captain Webb Dr TF4	17 F5
Captains Mdw TF1	17 F1
Careswell Gdns TF11	30 A5
Carlisle Cl TF1	6 D6
Carlton TF3	14 D5
Carmarthen Grn TF1	12 C2
Carnoustie Dr TF7	26 A2
Carvers Cl TF1	11 G4
Carvers Rd TF12	24 D5
Carwood TF3	22 C1
Castle Acre Rd TF1	6 D6
Castle Farm Way TF2	15 E5
Castle La TF1	13 E2
Castle Rd TF4	21 G2
Castle St TF1	13 E2
Castle Trading Est	
TF2	3 D1
Castle Vw TF1	13 F4
Castlecroft TF3	22 B1
Castlefields Way	
TF4,7	21 G3
Catherton TF3	18 C6
Catstree TF3	22 C1
Catterick Cl TF1	12 B1
Caughley Cl TF12	25 F6
Cavell Cl TF1	12 A1
Cavendish Cl TF2	13 H4
Caynton TF3	22 C2
Cecil Cl TF4	17 G3
Cedar Cl TF3	17 F1
Cedarwood Dr TF2	8 D4
Cemetery Rd TF4	17 F3
Central Av TF1	12 D4
Central Pk TF2	18 A1
Central Sq TF3	3 B5
Chainmakers Gate TF4	21 H3
Chalice Cl TF2	9 E4
Chancery Rd TF3	15 E5
Chantry Cl TF12	25 E3
Chapel Bank TF2	14 B2

Chapel La, Broseley TF12	24 D5
Chapel La, Telford TF3	21 H3
Chapel Rd, Ironbridge TF8	25 E1
Chapel Rd, Jackfield TF8	25 F2
Chapel St, Dawley TF4	17 F6
Chapel St, St Georges TF2	14 B5
Chapel Ter TF2	14 A2
Chapmans CI TF3	21 H2
Charborough Ct TF2	13 H4
Charlecote Pk TF3	17 E1
Charles Rd TF1	12 B5
Charles St TF2	14 B1
Charlton St, Oakengates TF2	13 H4
Charlton St, Wellington TF1	11 H3
Chartwell Rd TF1	12 C5
Chatford TF3	
Cheapside TF11	30 B4
Checkley La TF4	14 D4
Chelmarsh TF3	22 C2
Cheltenham Ct TF1	12 B1
Chepstow Dr TF1	12 B1
Cherrington TF3	22 B1
Cherry Gro TF3	17 G1
Cherry Tree Hill TF8	20 C5
Cherrybrook Dr TF12	24 D3
Cheshire CI TF7	25 G1
Cheshire Coppice La TF5	4 C4
Chesterfield Rd TF4	17 G5
Chesterton TF3	22 C1
Chestnut Dr, Trench TF2	7 H6
Chestnut Dr, Wellington TF1	11 F2
Chestnut Ter TF1	13 F2
Cheswell Dr TF10	27 A1
Chetwynd TF3	22 B2
Chetwynd End TF10	29 E3
Chetwynd Gro TF10	29 F2
Chetwynd Rd, Edgmond TF10	28 B2
Chetwynd Rd, Newport TF10	29 E1
Chichester Dr TF1	6 B5
Chilcombe Dr TF2	15 E6
Chillcott Dr TF7	22 B6
Chiltern Gdns TF4	17 F5
Chirbury TF3	22 B1
Chiswick Ct TF2	8 C4
Chockleys Dr TF1	12 C2
Chockleys Mdw TF1	12 C2
Christine Av TF1	11 H5
Church CI TF7	22 A6
Church Hill, Ironbridge TF8	24 D1
Church Hill, Lawley TF6	16 B3
Church Mdw, Newport TF10	9 G1
Church Mdw, Shifnal TF11	30 B4
Church Par TF2	13 H4
Church Rd, Coalbrookdale TF8	20 C5
Church Rd, Dawley TF4	17 G4
Church Rd, Donnington TF2	8 C6
Church Rd, Jackfield TF8	25 G3
Church Rd, Lilleshall TF10	9 F2
Church Rd, Malinslee TF3	3 A6
Church Rd, Snedshill TF2	14 B6
Church Rd, Trench TF2	7 H6
Church Sq TF10	29 F3
Church St, Broseley TF12	25 E5
Church St, Hadley TF1	13 E2
Church St, Madeley TF7	21 H6
Church St, Oakengates TF2	13 H5
Church St, St Georges TF2	14 C4
Church St, Shifnal TF11	30 B5
Church St, Wellington TF1	11 H3
Church Walk, Dawley TF4	21 G1
Church Walk, Donnington TF2	8 B5
Church Walk, Wellington TF1	12 A4
Churchill Dr TF2	14 A6
Churchill Rd TF1	12 B5
Churchward CI TF4	14 D5
Churchward Dr TF3	17 E2
Churchway TF3	22 C1
Churncote TF3	22 C1
Clanbrook TF3	22 C1
Claremont Mws TF1	11 H2
Clares Lane CI TF3	17 G1
Claverley Dr TF3	22 A2
Clematis Dr TF1	6 C6
Cleveland CI TF4	17 E6
Clift Cres TF1	11 G3
Clover Gro TF3	18 C6
Clowes Dr TF3	18 C5
Clun CI TF1	11 G1
Clunbury Rd TF1	11 F1
Clydesdale Dr TF4	17 E6
Coach Central TF3	3 B4
Coach Rd TF8	20 C5
Coachman Mdw TF1	5 G6
Coachwell CI TF3	17 H3
Coalbrookdale Rd TF6	20 A2
Coalford TF3	25 F2
Coalmoor La TF4	20 B1
Coalport CI TF12	25 F6
Coalport High St TF8	25 H3
Coalport Rd, Blists Hill TF8	25 H3
Coalport Rd, Broseley TF12	25 F6
Cobwell Rd TF12	24 D3
Cockshot La TF12	24 D4
Cockshutt Rd TF2	14 A4
Colemere Dr TF1	11 G2
College La TF1	12 A2
Collett Way TF2	14 C5
Colliers Way TF3	3 A2
Colliford CI TF2	15 E5
Collingwood Ct TF11	30 C2
Collins CI TF12	25 F6
Columbine Way TF2	8 D6
Combermere Dr TF1	11 G2
Commercial Way TF2	14 A5
Concorde TF4	17 F4
Coney Green Way TF1	5 H6
Coneybury Vw TF12	25 F5
Coniston Dr TF2	14 C6
Conners La TF10	28 A3
Connomara Mdw TF4	17 E6
Conroy Dr TF4	17 F4
Constable Dr TF5	5 F6
Constitution Hill TF1	12 A3
Cooke Dr TF4	21 H1
Cooper CI TF2	19 E1
Copper Beech Rd TF1	12 D4
Copperfield Dr TF2	8 C4
Coppice CI TF7	22 B6
Coppice Dr, Newport TF10	29 E1
Coppice Dr, Telford TF2	14 B3
Coppice Green La TF11	30 C4
Corbett CI TF4	21 F2
Cordingley Way TF2	14 B1
Corfield Cres TF4	13 H4
Cornbrook TF3	22 C1
Corndean Mdw TF3	17 E6
Cornflower Gro TF1	13 F5
Cornmell Lea TF10	29 F3
Cornwallis Dr TF11	30 C3
Coronation Cres TF3	23 A5
Coronation Dr TF2	8 C4
Corve Walk TF2	14 C2
Cote Rd TF5	5 F5
Cotswold Dr TF3	18 B5
Cottage CI TF7	22 B6
Cottage Dr TF11	30 B5
Cottage Farm CI TF7	22 A6
Cound CI TF7	11 G1
Court Rd TF7	22 A5
Court St TF7	22 A5
Court Works Ind Est TF7	22 A4
Courtland Dr TF2	13 H1
Crackshall La TF4	20 C3
Cranage Cres TF1	11 G3
Cranmere TF3	22 C1
Crescent Rd, Hadley TF1	12 C3
Crescent Rd, Wellington TF1	11 H2
Crest Rd TF2	14 D4
Cricketers La TF2	14 D4
Croft Fold TF4	17 F4
Crossbank TF3	22 C1
Crosskeys La TF1	12 D2
Crowdale Rd TF5	5 E5
Crown St, Dawley TF4	17 G6
Crown St, Wellington TF1	11 H3
Cuckoo Oak End TF7	22 B5
Cuckoos Rest TF4	21 H3
Culmington TF3	18 B6
Cumberland CI TF12	24 D4
Cumberland Mws TF1	12 B2
Curie Cft TF1	6 A6
Curlew Dr TF1	12 C2
Curriers La TF11	30 C3
Cygnet Dr TF3	22 B3
Cyril Hayward Ct TF1	13 E2
Daddlebrook TF3	18 C4
Daisy Bank Dr TF2	14 C3
Dalby CI TF1	12 B1
Dale Acre Way, Telford TF3	3 D6
Dale Acre Way, Telford TF3	3 C4
Dale Rd TF8	20 C6
Dalebrook Dr TF2	8 D6
Dalefield Dr TF5	4 D6
Dalelands TF3	3 D5
Dalford Ct TF3	3 C5
Dallamoor TF3	18 C3
Damson Dr TF3	13 F6
Danesford TF3	18 B3
Daniels Cross TF10	29 G2
Darby Rd TF8	20 B4
Dark La, Broseley TF12	25 E5
Dark La, Telford TF3	18 C3
Dark Lane Dr TF3	17 H4
Darliston TF3	18 C4
Darwin Rd TF1	11 H2
Dashwood Dr TF1	5 G6
Davenham Walk TF3	17 E2
Davenport Dr TF5	5 E5
Dawley Bank TF4	17 F3
Dawley Green Way TF3	17 G3
Dawley Rd TF1	12 B4
Daywell TF3	18 C3
Dean CI TF4	14 D5
Dean St*, Telford Shopping Centre TF3	3 B4
Dee CI TF1	11 H1
Deepdale TF3	18 B3
Deepfield Rd TF4	21 F1
Deer Park Dr TF10	29 E1
Deer Park Rd TF1	11 G1
Deer Park Way TF4	14 D2
Deercote TF3	3 C5
Delamere CI TF3	17 E1
Delbury Ct TF3	3 C5
Delphside TF7	25 E5
Derwent Dr TF2	14 C6
Deuxhill CI TF4	17 F4
Dickens Rd TF2	14 A1
Dinchope Dr TF3	18 C3
Dinthill TF3	18 C4
Doddington TF3	18 C3
Doddlecote CI TF3	22 A1
Dodmoor Grange TF3	18 B5
Dog in the Lane TF6	16 B4
Domas Way TF4	17 F4
Donnerville CI TF7	11 F1
Donnerville Dr TF5	11 F2
Donnerville Gdns TF5	11 F1
Donnington Dr TF2	8 A1
Donnington Way TF2	8 B2
Donnington Wood Bsns Pk TF2	14 C2
Donnington Wood Way TF2	8 C4
Dorchester Dr TF2	9 E6
Dorran PI TF2	14 B5
Doseley Ind Est TF4	21 E1
Doseley Rd TF4	17 F6
Dothill Ct*, Severn Dr TF1	11 G1
Dove Ct TF8	25 E1
Dovedale Fold TF3	17 H5
Dovehouse Ct TF12	25 E5
Dover Dr TF1	6 D6
Downemead TF3	3 D5
Downton CI TF3	3 D5
Drapers Ct TF1	11 H2
Draycott TF3	18 C4
Drayton Rd TF11	30 C2
Drayton Way TF4	17 F4
Drovers Way TF10	29 G2
Drummery La TF6	10 C3
Drummond CI TF12	21 E5
Duckett Dr TF4	17 F6
Dudmaston TF3	18 C3
Duffryn TF3	3 D4
Duke St, Broseley TF12	24 D4
Duke St, Telford TF1	11 H3
Dukes Hill TF2	13 H6
Dukes PI TF2	14 B4
Dukes St TF2	14 C4
Dukes Way TF2	14 C4
Dungarven Dr TF10	29 E4
Dunlin CI TF1	12 C2
Dunmaster Way TF3	22 A2
Dunsheath TF3	3 D4
Dunstone TF3	18 C3
Durrant Rd TF2	14 C5
Duxmore Way TF4	17 F4
Dyas CI TF11	30 B5
Dyas Mws TF11	30 B5
Eagle Ct*, Crescent Rd TF1	11 H2
Earls Dr TF4	21 H3
Earlswood Dr TF7	25 G1
East Av TF2	8 B5
East Rd TF2	13 H6
East Vw TF6	10 C2
East Vw*, Humber La TF2	7 H2
Easthope Rd TF12	24 D3
Eastwood Dr TF2	14 C1
Eaton Cres TF2	14 A5
Edgmond Rd TF10	29 E2
Edinburgh Rd TF2	14 D4
Edith CI TF3	21 H2
Edward Parry Ct TF4	17 G3
Eglantine CI TF2	8 D5
Eider Dr TF1	6 B6
Elderberry CI TF3	17 G1
Eleanors CI TF4	21 G3
Eliot CI TF3	18 C6
Elizabeth Cres TF12	24 D4
Elkington CI TF10	29 E4
Ellesmere Ct TF10	29 F4
Ellis Peters Dr TF3	21 H2
Ellwand Ct TF4	21 G1
Elm CI TF10	29 F5
Elm Way TF2	13 G1
Elmhurst Coppice TF2	8 D4
Elmpark Dr TF1	11 F2
Elmsdale Cres TF5	5 E6
Eltham TF3	15 F5
Elvin CI TF4	21 E1
Ely CI TF2	15 F6
Emral Rise TF1	11 H1
Ennerdale CI TF2	14 C6
Epsom Ct TF1	12 B2
Ercall CI TF2	13 H1
Ercall Gdns TF1	11 H4
Ercall La TF1	11 G5
Ercall Vw TF1	13 E6
Espley CI TF1	11 H1
Essex Chase TF2	14 D5
Euston Way TF3	3 D3
Everglade Rd TF2	14 D5
Ewart Rd TF2	8 B6
Exeter Dr TF1	12 A2
Eyton PI TF4	17 G5
Eyton Rd TF4	17 G5
Eyton Vw TF1	5 H6
Fair Oak TF10	29 F2
Fairburn Rd TF3	18 B5
Fairfield Ct TF1	11 H2
Fairways Dr TF7	25 G1
Fallow Deer Lawn TF10	29 F1
Fallow Rd TF5	5 F5
Far Vallens TF1	13 E3
Farm CI TF7	22 B6
Farm Gro TF10	28 D4
Farm La TF4	16 D5
Farm Lane Bungalows TF2	8 B6
Farm Lodge Gro TF3	17 H4
Farmstead Ct TF1	11 F5
Farriers Grn, Newport TF10	29 H3
Farriers Grn, Telford TF1	17 E3
Fellows CI TF4	21 G2
Fence Rd TF4	17 E5
Fenns Cres TF2	14 B3
Ferndale Dr TF2	18 D6
Fernwood CI TF1	5 G2
Ferriday CI TF7	21 E5
Ferry Rd TF8	25 H3
Festival Gdns TF1	12 B4
Field CI TF4	17 G1
Field La TF1	23 H4
Fieldfare Way TF4	21 H2
Fieldhouse Dr TF2	8 C4
Fielding CI TF12	25 F4
Fifth Av TF2	13 H6
Finchale Av TF2	15 E5
Finger Rd TF4	17 E3
Finsbury Dr TF2	15 E5
Fireclay Dr TF2	14 B4
Firecrest Dr TF1	12 A2
First Av TF2	14 A4
Fishers Lock TF10	29 F3
Flag Leasow TF7	25 G4
Fleming Ct TF1	12 B5
Floyer La TF12	24 C4
Forbes CI TF7	21 E5
Ford Rd TF10	29 E1
Forest CI TF5	5 C
Forester Gro TF1	12 A
Forester Rd TF12	25
Foresters CI TF4	16 D
Forge Retail Pk TF3	3 A
Forgegate TF3	
Forsythia CI TF2	15
Forton Glade TF10	29
Forton Rd TF10	29
Fosters Foel TF4	21 F
Foundry CI TF2	14 A
Foundry Ct*, Foundry La TF12	25
Fountain Dr TF2	14
Fourth Av TF2	13
Fowler CI TF1	11
Fox Av TF2	14
Fox La TF12	24
Foxglove Rise TF3	18
Foxs Covert TF5	5
Frame La TF4	14
Freeston Av TF4	14
Frizes Leasowe TF2	13
Frome Way TF2	14
Fuchsia CI TF2	15
Furnace La TF2	8
Furnace Rd TF2	14
Fylingdales Dr TF4	21
Gainsborough Way TF5	5
Garbett Rd TF4	13
Garden CI TF2	13
Garfield Rd TF3	13
Gatcombe Way TF2	15

Lineton Cl TF2	14 A1
Linley Dr TF3	22 B2
Linnet Gate TF1	5 F5
Lintin Cl TF5	5 E5
Lion St TF2	14 A4
Little Cft TF2	13 H4
Little Eyton Fold TF4	17 G5
Little Hales Rd TF10	29 G6
Little Meadow Cl TF5	4 D6
Lloyds Head TF8	25 F2
Lodge Cl TF11	30 B6
Lodge La, Benthall TF12	24 C5
Lodge La, Ironbridge TF8	24 D1
Lodge Rd, Donnington TF2	14 C1
Lodge Rd, St Georges TF2	14 C5
Lodgewood La TF2	14 D4
London Rd TF2	14 C5
Long Lane Dr TF7	21 E5
Long Mdw TF3	18 B6
Longford Rd TF8	28 B5
Longford Rise TF1	12 A1
Longmynd Ct TF1	11 G1
Longnor Rd TF1	11 F1
Longwithy La TF10	28 A1
Lord Murray Dr TF7	21 F4
Lords Dr TF2	14 C4
Lovell Cl TF11	30 C2
Low Valley Cl TF1	13 E3
Lowe Ct TF1	12 A3
Lower Bar TF10	29 E3
Lower Brook TF3	17 F2
Lower Dingle TF7	25 G1
Lower Park Dr TF1	5 G6
Lower Wood TF3	17 F2
Loweswater Cl TF2	14 C6
Lowry Cl TF5	5 F5
Lucerne Cl TF1	12 D2
Ludford Dr TF3	22 A1
Ludlow Dr TF3	22 A1
Lydbury Cl TF3	22 B2
Lyndhurst Dr TF2	13 H1
Lytham Grn TF2	9 E5
Maddocks TF7	21 H6
Maddocks Ct TF1	11 H4
Madebrook Cl TF7	22 C6
Madeley Rd TF8	25 E2
Madeley Wood Vw TF7	25 G1
Mafeking Dr TF2	14 B2
Mafeking Rd TF1	12 D3
Mafeking Ter TF2	14 B2
Magna Cl TF4	21 G1
Magnolia Dr TF3	17 F1
Main Rd TF3	13 G5
Majestic Way TF4	21 G3
Malinsgate TF3	3 A4
Mallard Cl TF3	22 B3
Mallory Dr TF3	21 H2
Malvern Cres TF4	21 F2
Manchester Dr TF1	6 B6
Mannerley La TF3	13 F6
Manor Cl TF11	30 B5
Manor Dr TF2	14 B5
Manor Gdns TF4	21 G1
Manor Rd, Arleston TF1	12 B5
Manor Rd, Hadley TF1	12 D2
Manor Rd, Newport TF10	28 A2
Manor Rd, Telford TF4	21 F1
Manor Rise TF1	12 C5
Manse Cl TF1	12 D2
Manse Rd TF1	12 D2
Mansell Rd TF1	11 G3
Maple Cl, Shifnal TF11	30 B3
Maple Cl, Telford TF2	13 H2
Maple Wood TF3	18 B6
Margaret Ct TF1	12 D4
Marigold Cl TF1	13 F5
Market Pl TF11	30 B4
Market Sq TF1	11 H3
Market St, Oakengates TF2	14 A4
Market St, Wellington TF1	11 H3
Marlborough Way TF3	17 E1
Marlow Dr TF2	14 A1
Marquis Ter TF2	14 A6
Marrions Hill TF2	14 B5
Marsh Meadow Cl TF1	5 F6
Marshbrook Way TF2	8 C4
Mart Av TF2	14 B5
Martin Rd TF1	11 H3
Martingale Way TF4	17 E3
Marton Dr TF1	11 G1
Mason Dr TF7	21 G5
Masons Pl TF10	29 F2
Matlock Av TF4	17 H4
Maurice Lee Av TF1	13 H4
Mayfair Gro TF2	15 E5
Mayfield TF7	21 H6
Maynards Cft TF10	29 G2
Maypole Rd TF12	24 D3
Maythorne Cl TF1	26 B1
McCormick Dr TF1	5 G5
McLean Dr TF2	14 D5
Mead Way TF1	30 C4
Meadcroft TF7	21 H6
Meadow Brook Cl TF7	22 A6
Meadow Cl, Madeley TF7	26 B1
Meadow Cl, Trench TF2	13 G1
Meadow Dr TF11	30 C2
Meadow Rd, Dawley TF4	17 F5
Meadow Rd, Donnington TF2	8 C4
Meadow Rd, Newport TF10	29 G3
Meadow Rd, Wellington TF1	11 F5
Meadow View Cl TF10	29 G3
Meadow View Rd TF10	29 G3
Meadowdale Dr TF5	4 D6
Meadowlea TF7	21 H6
Meadowsweet Dr TF2	14 D6
Medlar Cl TF3	13 G6
Meese Cl TF1	11 H1
Melbourne Cl TF4	17 H5
Mellor Cl TF7	25 G1
Melrose Gdns TF1	11 G4
Mendip Cl TF4	21 F2
Mentone Cres TF10	28 B2
Mercia Dr TF1	12 B2
Mercian Ct TF11	30 B3
Mere Cl, Newport TF10	29 F2
Mere Cl, Shifnal TF11	30 C5
Mere Gro TF5	5 G5
Merevale Rd TF3	17 E2
Merganser Cl TF1	6 B6
Merridale Cres TF1	12 A2
Merrington Rd TF2	9 E3
Meyrick Rd TF1	11 H2
Middle Rd TF2	14 A2
Mill Bank TF1	11 H3
Mill Farm Dr TF3	18 C5
Mill La, Broseley TF12	24 D5
Mill La, Madeley TF7	22 A6
Mill La, Shifnal TF11	23 G6
Mill La, Wellington TF1	12 A4
Mill Way TF2	7 H6
Millard Cl TF1	5 G5
Millers Way TF2	9 E4
Millfields Rd TF1	12 B4
Millman Gro TF4	16 D3
Millstream Way TF1	12 C1
Millward Cl TF2	8 A5
Milners Ct TF4	17 F3
Milners La TF4	17 F3
Milton Dr TF7	21 G6
Mimosa Cl TF7	26 A2
Mitchel Way TF7	5 G6
Moat Cft TF11	30 B5
Moat Cl TF1	5 G6
Mole Vw TF5	5 F5
Monet Cl TF5	5 F5
Montgomery Mws TF1	6 C5
Montgomery Rd TF1	11 G3
Moor Rd TF4	17 G5
Moorfield La TF10	29 E5
Moorland Dr TF2	14 D6
Moorland Rd TF10	29 E4
Morden Cl TF2	14 B5
Morgan Way TF1	13 E4
Morris Dr TF2	8 B5
Morton Cl TF4	17 F5
Morville Dr TF1	11 G1
Mosclay Rd TF2	14 C5
Moss Rd TF2	14 B2
Mossey Green Way TF1	13 G5
Mossey Grn TF2	13 G6
Mound Way TF7	21 G6
Mount Gilbert TF1	12 A5
Mount Pleasant TF2	13 H6
Mount Pleasant Dr TF3	22 A3
Mount Pleasant Rd TF7	22 B6
Mount Rd TF4	17 G4
Mount Side TF1	13 E5
Mount View Rd TF2	13 H5
Mountbatten Cl TF11	30 C2
Mounts Cl TF7	22 B6
Mulberry Cl TF10	29 F5
Mulberry Ct TF1	12 D2
Mullinder Dr TF2	13 H6
Musk Rose Cl TF2	8 D5
Muxton La TF2	8 D3
Myford TF4	20 D1
Nabb Cl TF2	14 B4
Naird La, Shifnal TF11	19 E4
Naird La, Telford TF3	18 C6
Near Vallens TF1	12 A4
Nelson Ct, Shifnal TF11	30 C2
Nelson Ct, Telford TF1	12 A4
Nelson Way TF2	9 E3
Nevil Rd TF1	11 G2
Neville Gro TF5	5 E5
New Bri TF8	25 F2
New Bridge Rd TF8	25 E2
New Church Cl TF1	12 A4
New Church Rd TF1	12 A4
New Hall Rd TF1	12 A3
New Rd, Dawley TF4	17 G6
New Rd, Donnington TF2	8 C5
New Rd, Ironbridge TF8	24 D1
New Rd, Madeley TF7	21 H6
New Rd, Oakengates TF2	14 A3
New River Cl TF1	5 G6
New Row TF4	16 D5
New Row*, Telford Shopping Centre TF3	3 B4
New St, Dawley TF4	17 G6
New St, Newport TF10	29 F3
New St, Oakengates TF2	13 H4
New St, St Georges TF2	14 B4
New St, Wellington TF1	11 H3
New St*, Telford Shopping Centre TF3	3 B4
New Town TF4	17 G5
New Trench Rd TF2	7 G6
New Works La TF6	16 B2
Newbrookdale TF1	12 D2
Newcomen Way TF7	21 E6
Newfield Cl TF11	30 B3
Newfield Ct TF2	13 H2
Newfield Dr TF1	13 H2
Newlands Rd TF2	14 A5
Newport By-Pass TF10	29 G1
Newport Cres TF11	30 C3
Newport Rd, Newport TF10	28 B2
Newport Rd, Shifnal TF11	30 C3
Newtonmere Dr TF1	11 G2
Newtown TF10	29 E5
Nickless Way TF4	17 F4
Nightingale Way TF1	6 B6
Norbroom Ct TF10	29 G2
Norbroom Dr TF10	29 G2
Norfield Vw TF3	18 C5
North Rd TF1	11 G2
North Sherwood St*, Telford Shopping Centre TF3	3 B4
North St TF2	3 B4
Northwood Ter TF3	18 A6
Norton Dr TF3	22 A2
Norwich Dr TF3	18 C6
Oak Av TF10	29 F5
Oak Cl TF7	22 B5
Oak Rd TF3	17 F1
Oakengates Rd TF2	14 B1
Oakfield Rd, Shifnal TF11	30 B3
Oakfield Rd, Telford TF5	5 F4
Oaklands Dr TF2	7 H6
Oaks Cres TF1	11 F5
Oakwood Dr TF2	7 H6
Okehampton Rd TF1	6 C5
Old Coppice Grange TF3	17 G1
Old Farm La TF10	9 G1
Old Hall Cl TF1	12 B4
Old Nursery Cl TF7	21 H5
Old Office Cl TF4	17 E4
Old Office Rd TF4	17 E4
Old Park Rd TF2	13 H6
Old Park Way TF3	17 G2
Old Vicarage Rd TF4	21 G1
Old Wharf TF3	17 H4
Oldcroft TF2	13 H4
Oldfield Rd TF4	21 H1
Oleander Cl TF3	13 F6
Oliver Ct TF1	11 H2
Onslow Dr TF1	11 G2
Ony Gro TF2	14 C2
Orchard Cl, Newport TF10	29 F6
Orchard Cl, Telford TF1	13 E5
Orchard La TF8	25 E1
Orchard Rd TF11	30 C3
Orchard Way TF1	12 A4
Orchid Cl TF2	8 D6
Orleton La TF1	11 G3
Orleton Ter TF1	11 G3
Ormsdale Cl TF2	8 D4
Osprey Gro TF1	6 B5
Osterley Gro TF2	9 E4
Oval Cl TF2	14 D4
Overdale TF3	13 E6
Owen Cl TF4	22 D1
Oxford Rd TF4	17 G5
Oxford St TF2	14 A4
Oxlip Cl TF2	8 D5
Paddock Cl TF1	11 G2
Paddock Ct TF4	17 G6
Paddock La TF11	23 F4
Padmans Alley TF12	24 D4
Pageant Cl TF1	21 G2
Panorama TF2	14 A4
Paradise TF8	20 C6
Pargeter Cl TF3	21 H2
Parish Cl TF4	21 F1
Parish Dr TF4	13 E2
Park Av TF7	21 H6
Park Cl TF2	14 C5
Park Ct, Shifnal TF11	30 B5
Park Ct, Telford TF7	21 F5
Park End TF10	29 F1
Park La, Madeley TF7	21 F5
Park La, Old Park TF3	17 G1
Park La, Shifnal TF11	30 C5
Park Rd, Donnington TF2	8 B6
Park Rd, Malinslee TF4	17 F3
Park St, Madeley TF7	21 H6
Park St, Shifnal TF11	30 B4
Park St, Wellington TF1	11 H2
Park Vw TF12	24 D5
Parkdale TF1	12 D1
Parklands TF1	11 G2
Parkway TF7	21 G6
Partridge Cl TF1	12 A1
Pasmore Cl TF3	21 H3
Pasteur Dr TF1	6 A6
Pave La TF10	29 G5
Pavilion Gro TF2	14 D
Pearson Rd TF2	14 A
Pemberton Rd TF5	11 E
Pembridge Cl TF2	8 C
Pembroke Dr TF1	12 A
Pen y Bryn Way TF10	29 F
Pendil Cl TF1	11 F
Penistone Cl TF2	8 C
Peregrine Way TF1	6 A
Perivale Gdns TF2	9 E
Perry Ct TF1	11 H
Peters La TF1	21 G
Peveril Bank TF4	17 G
Picasso Cl TF5	5 F
Pickering Rd TF2	14 A
Pickford Pl TF2	13 H
Pickstock Cl TF3	22 B
Pickwick Ct TF11	30 C
Picton Cl TF2	14 C
Pine Vw TF2	8 D
Pinefields TF11	30 C
Pinewood Av TF2	7 H
Pinewoods TF10	29 E
Pintail Dr TF1	6 B
Pipers La TF10	28 A
Pitchford Dr TF2	14 D
Plant Cl TF4	17 F
Plough La TF10	29 G
Plough Rd, Trench TF2	14 A
Plough Rd, Wellington TF1	11 H
Ploughmans Cft TF10	29 G
Plover Gate TF1	5 F
Poachers Gate TF4	21 H
Pool Cl TF2	13 G
Pool Farm La TF1	6 E
Pool Hill TF4	17
Pool Hill Rd TF4	17
Pool Mdw TF1	13 E
Pool Rd TF2	13 C
Pool Side TF4	16 D
Pool Vw TF4	16 D
Poplar Cl TF7	22
Poplar Dr TF1	11
Poppy Dr TF2	8 B
Porchester Cl TF1	6 B
Portland Dr TF3	17
Portley Rd TF4	17
Portobello Cl TF3	17
Pound La TF12	25
Powder La TF1	11
Powell Pl TF10	29
Powell Rd TF2	14
Powis Dr TF1	11
Powis Pl TF4	17
Prestage Cl TF12	25
Preston Gro TF2	7
Primmer Rd TF2	8
Primrose Dr TF10	29
Primrose Gro TF1	12
Prince Andrew Dr TF3	17
Prince Charles Cres TF3	17
Prince Edward Cres TF3	17
Prince St TF7	22
Princes End TF4	17
Princes St TF1	12
Princess Anne Gdns TF4	12
Princess Av TF1	12
Princess Gdns TF10	29
Priors Gate TF1	18
Priorslee Av TF2	12
Priorslee Rd, Shifnal TF11	19
Priorslee Rd, Telford TF2	14
Priorslee Trading Est TF2	
Priorslee Village TF2	18
Priory Cl TF1	11
Priory Rd TF2	13
Proctors Pl TF2	14
Prospect Rd TF1	12
Punta Verde Dr TF7	26
Purbeck Dale TF4	17
Purton Wood Vw TF2	

Tan Bank, Newport TF10 29 F3
Tan Bank, Telford TF1 11 H3
Tanglewood Cl TF11 30 B6
Tarbach Cl TF12 25 F6
Teagues Cres TF2 13 G1
Teal Cl TF3 22 B3
Teawell Cl TF3 17 F2
Tee Lake Blvd TF1 5 F6
Teece Dr TF2 18 D1
Telford Bridge Retail Pk TF3 3 A3
Telford Rd, Malinslee TF4 17 G4
Telford Rd, Wellington TF1 11 G5
Telford Science & Technology Pk TF11 19 E5
Telford Shopping Centre TF3 3 B4
Telford Way TF3 3 D3
Teme Av TF1 11 F1
Tenbury Dr TF2 7 H6
Teresa Way TF1 12 B1
Tern Cl TF4 21 F3
Tern Way TF1 11 G1
The Avenue, Broseley TF12 24 A3
The Avenue, Telford TF6 10 C2
The Beeches TF5 5 E6
The Bentlands TF12 24 C4
The Border*, Telford Shopping Centre TF3 3 B4
The Brambles TF3 17 F2
The Bungalows TF2 8 C4
The Cloisters TF2 13 H3
The Close, Newport TF10 29 E6
The Close, Telford TF8 20 B4
The Common TF2 8 C6
The Coppice TF3 17 H1
The Court TF7 26 A2
The Crescent, Newport TF10 29 F6
The Crescent, Telford TF2 8 C5
The Crest TF3 17 H1
The Crofts TF5 21 E5
The Dale TF10 29 F6
The Delph TF3 18 B6
The Fields TF2 8 D5
The Finger TF4 21 G1
The Foxes TF7 26 A1
The Grove, Shifnal TF11 30 C5
The Grove, Telford TF1 12 D1
The Grove Est TF2 14 B5
The Hay TF3 17 F2
The Incline TF1 13 E5
The Knowle TF8 25 F3
The Larches TF10 29 E4
The Lawns TF1 11 H2
The Ley TF4 17 G6
The Lindens TF1 30 B4
The Lloyds TF8 25 F2
The Maltings TF1 11 G3
The Meadow TF2 13 H5
The Meadows TF4 16 D3
The Mines TF12 24 D3
The Nabb TF2 14 B3
The Parade, Donnington TF2 8 B5
The Parade, Wellington TF1 11 H3
The Pippins TF3 18 B6
The Rock TF3 17 F1
The Rookery TF7 22 A6
The Savannahs TF1 5 H6
The Shires TF2 18 C1
The Spinney, Newport TF10 29 F6
The Spinney, Telford TF2 8 D4
The Square TF8 24 D2
The Stables TF2 9 E4
The Stocking TF4 21 E3
The Timbers TF2 14 B4
The Wharfage TF8 24 C1
The Woodlands, Oakengates TF2 14 A3
The Woodlands, Wellington TF1 13 F6
Thetford Chase*, Telford Shopping Centre TF3 3 B4
Third Av TF2 3 B1
Thirlmere Gro TF2 14 C6
Thistle Cl TF3 18 C5
Thornton Park Av TF2 9 E4
Toll Rd TF1 12 C5
Tom Morgan Cl TF4 16 D3
Tom Wedge Ct TF12 25 G5
Tontine Hill TF8 24 D1
Town Wells TF3 17 F1
Townsend Cft TF2 8 C4
Trafalgar Cl TF2 8 C3
Trench Cl TF2 13 G1
Trench Lock TF1 13 F1
Trench Rd TF2 13 F1
Trenleigh Gdns TF2 13 H1
Trevithick Cl TF7 21 F5
Trinity Rd TF4 21 F1
Trinity Vw TF2 13 H5
Troon Way TF7 26 A2
Tuckers Pl TF10 29 F3
Tudor Cl TF10 29 G2
Tudor Mdw TF2 13 G1
Tudor Way TF11 30 C4
Turbervill Cl TF2 14 C3
Turners La TF10 28 A3
Turnpike Ct TF2 14 C3
Turnstone Dr TF1 12 C2
Turreff Av TF2 8 B5
Tweedale Cres TF7 22 A5
Tweedale Ct TF7 22 A4
Tweedale Ind Est TF7 22 A5
Tweedale North TF7 22 A4
Tweedale South TF7 22 A5
Tynsley Ct TF7 22 A6
Tynsley Ter TF7 22 A5

Ullswater Cl TF2 14 C6
Underhill Cl TF10 29 F3
Undertrees Cl TF1 5 G6
Underwood TF12 25 E4
Union Ct TF2 13 E2
Union Rd, Oakengates TF2 14 A3
Union Rd, Wellington TF1 11 H4
Union St TF1 13 E2
Uplands Av TF2 13 H4
Upper Bar TF10 29 F4
Upper Dingle TF7 25 G1
Upper Rd TF7 25 H1
Upper Wood TF3 17 F2
Urban Gdns TF1 12 B4
Urban Rd TF2 14 A3
Urban Villas TF2 14 B4
Urban Way TF1 12 B4

Valley Rd, Arleston TF1 12 B5
Valley Rd, Overdale TF3 13 E6
Vauxhall Cres TF10 29 E4
Vauxhall Ter TF10 29 E4
Verbena Way TF7 26 A2
Vicar St TF2 13 H5
Vicarage Dr TF11 30 B5
Vicarage Gro TF4 17 F6
Victoria Av, Ketley TF1 12 D4
Victoria Av, Wellington TF1 12 A3
Victoria Ct, Shifnal TF11 30 B4
Victoria Ct, Telford TF1 13 E2
Victoria Pk TF10 29 F2
Victoria Rd, Madeley TF7 21 H5
Victoria Rd, Shifnal TF11 30 B4
Victoria Rd, Wellington TF1 11 H3
Victoria St TF1 11 H3
Viewlands Dr TF2 7 H6
Villa Ct TF7 21 H5
Village Cl TF2 13 H4
Village Gdns TF2 18 C1
Village Way TF2 13 G4
Vineyard Dr, Newport TF10 29 F3
Vineyard Dr, Telford TF1 11 H2
Vineyard Pl TF1 11 G2
Vineyard Rd, Newport TF10 29 F3
Vineyard Rd, Telford TF1 11 H3
Violet Cl TF2 8 D5
Viscount Av TF4 21 H3

Wade Rd TF2 14 A1
Wadham Cl TF1 12 A2
Waggoners Fold TF3 17 H4
Wagtail Dr TF1 21 H3
Wains Cl TF3 17 F2
Walder Cl TF4 17 F4
Walker Cres TF2 14 B4
Walker St TF1 11 H3
Wallshead Way TF10 29 F6
Walney Ct TF7 21 F5
Walnut Cl, Newport TF10 29 F5
Walnut Cl, Telford TF4 21 H3
Walsh Cl TF2 14 D5
Waltondale TF7 21 G5
Wantage TF7 21 G4
Warrensway TF7 21 E6
Warwick Way TF1 6 D6
Water La TF10 29 E3
Waterford Dr TF10 29 E5
Waterloo Cl TF1 13 E3
Waterloo Rd, Ketley TF1 13 E2
Waterloo Rd, Wellington TF1 12 A3
Waterloo St TF8 25 E2
Waterlow Ct TF1 15 F5
Waterside Mws TF10 29 E3
Watling St TF1 12 B4
Waverley TF7 21 H5
Wavertree Cl TF2 14 B5
Waxhill Cl TF4 14 C1
Wayside TF7 21 G5
Wealdstone TF7 21 F5
Weavers Rise TF2 13 G6
Webb Cres TF4 17 F6
Wedgewood Cres TF1 12 D3
Weir Gdns TF1 13 E2
Wellington Ct TF1 11 H4
Wellington Rd, Admaston TF5 5 E6
Wellington Rd, Coalbrookdale TF8 20 C5
Wellington Rd, Donnington TF2 8 A5
Wellington Rd, Horsehay TF4 16 C5
Wellington Rd, Lilleshall TF2 9 E3
Wellington Rd, Newport TF10 29 E6
Wellsfield TF2 21 G5
Wellswood Av TF2 3 B1
Wenlock Ct TF7 21 F5
Wenlock Dr TF10 29 E4
Wentworth Dr TF4 21 G3
Wesley Cres TF11 30 B5
Wesley Dr TF2 13 H5
Wesley Rd TF8 25 E1
West Av TF2 8 A6
West Centre Way TF4 17 E2
West Rd, Oakengates TF2 13 G5
West St TF2 14 B5
West View Ter TF7 21 G6
Westbourne TF7 21 F6
Westcroft Walk TF2 14 C5
Westerdale Cl TF4 21 F1
Westerkirk Dr TF7 21 G6
Western Rise TF1 12 D4
Westminster Way TF2 15 E5
Westmorland Mws TF1 12 C2
Weston Cl TF11 30 C2
Weston Dr TF1 11 G2
Weybourne Walk TF2 9 E5
Weybridge TF7 21 E5
Weyman Rd TF1 11 G2
Wharf Cl TF2 14 B4
Wheatfield Dr TF11 30 B3
Wheatley Cres TF1 12 D1
Wheeldale Cl TF4 21 E1
Whimbrel Cl TF1 12 C2
Whinchat Cl TF1 12 A1
Whitchurch Dr TF1 5 G5
Whitchurch Rd TF1 5 H6
White Horse Cl TF4 17 F4
Whitebeam Cl TF3 17 G1
Whitehall Gdns TF12 25 E5
Whitemere Dr TF1 11 G2
Whiteway Dr TF5 5 E5
Whitmore Cl TF12 25 F6
Whitworth Dr TF3 18 B5
Wicket Cl TF2 14 D4
Widewaters Cl TF4 21 G3
Wigeon Gro TF1 6 B6
Wigmores TF7 21 G5
Wild Thyme Dr TF2 8 D5
Wildwood TF7 21 F5
Wilkinson Av TF12 25 E4
Willetts Way TF4 17 E4
Williams Rd TF2 8 B2
Willmoor La TF10 27 C2
Willow Bank TF4 21 H3
Willow Rd TF2 14 A4
Willowdale TF11 30 B3
Willowfield TF7 21 G4
Wilmere Ct TF2 21 F5
Wilton Ct TF7 21 F5
Winchester Dr TF2 9 E5
Windermere Dr TF2 14 C6
Windsor Cres TF12 24 D4
Windsor Flats*, Windsor Rd TF1 12 C4
Windsor Pl TF4 17 F6
Windsor Rd, Arleston TF1 12 C4
Windsor Rd, Dawley TF4 17 F6
Winifreds Dr TF1 8 B6
Winston Dr TF2 8 C5
Withington Cl TF2 13 H?
Withybrook TF7 21 E?
Withywood Dr, Malinslee TF3 17 H
Withywood Dr, Telford TF3 3 A
Wizard Way TF4 21 G
Wolverley Ct TF7 21 F
Wombridge Hill TF2 13 G
Wombridge Rd TF2 7 H
Wombridge Way TF2 13 G
Wood Cl TF2 14 B
Woodbine Dr TF2 8 D
Woodcroft TF7 21 G
Woodford Gro TF5 5 E
Woodhall Cl TF5 5 E
Woodhouse TF2 8 A
Woodhouse Central TF3 3 A
Woodhouse Cres TF2 8 A
Woodhouse La, Horsehay TF4 20 D
Woodhouse La, Telford TF2 14 D
Woodhouse La, Telford TF2 15 G
Woodhouse La, Telford TF2 15 E
Woodhouse Rd TF12 24 D
Woodland Villas TF2 14 A
Woodlands Av TF1 11
Woodlands Cl TF12 24 D
Woodlands Grn TF12 24 D
Woodlands La TF4 20 D
Woodlands Rd TF8 25 H
Woodpecker Cl TF1 6 C
Woodridge Cl TF10 28
Woodrows TF7 21 C
Woodrush Hth TF3 17 C
Woodside TF8 20
Woodside Av TF2 21
Woodside Cl TF1 13 H
Woodside Rd TF1 13
Woodspring Gro TF2 9
Woodwell TF1 13 C
Woollam Rd TF1 12
Woolpack Cl TF11 30
Worcester Rd TF4 17
Wordsworth Way TF2 14
Worfe Cl TF3 18
Worfe Rd TF11 30
Wrekin Av TF10 29
Wrekin Cl TF2 13
Wrekin Ct TF1 11
Wrekin Dr TF2 8
Wrekin Rd TF1 11
Wrekin Retail Pk TF1 12
Wrekin Vw, Madeley TF7 25
Wrekin Vw, Wrockwardine TF6 10
Wrekin Walk*, Telford Shopping Centre TF3 3
Wrens Nest La TF1 13
Wrockwardine Rd TF6 13
Wrockwardine Wood Way TF2 13
Wroxeter Way TF3 22
Wych Elm Dr TF5 5
Wyke La TF12 24
Wyke Rise TF7 12
Wyke Way TF11 30
Wyndham Gro TF2 18
Wyvern TF7 21

Yates Way TF2 13
Yellowstone Cl TF2 14
Yew Tree Ct TF11 30
Yew Tree Dr TF10 9
Yew Tree Rd TF7 25
York Rd TF2 11